Animal Horns

By Connor Stratton

level 2
little blue readers

www.littlebluehousebooks.com

Little Blue House is distributed by North Star Editions:
sales@northstareditions.com | 888-417-0195

Produced for Little Blue House by Red Line Editorial.

Photographs ©: iStockphoto, cover, 4, 7 (top), 7 (bottom), 9 (top), 9 (bottom), 11 (top), 11 (bottom), 12 (top), 12 (bottom), 15 (top), 15 (bottom), 17 (top), 17 (bottom), 18 (top), 18 (bottom), 21 (top), 21 (bottom), 24 (top left), 24 (top right), 24 (bottom left), 24 (bottom right); Shutterstock Images, 22–23

Library of Congress Control Number: 2020900815

ISBN
978-1-64619-176-5 (hardcover)
978-1-64619-210-6 (paperback)
978-1-64619-278-6 (ebook pdf)
978-1-64619-244-1 (hosted ebook)

Printed in the United States of America
Mankato, MN
082020

About the Author

Connor Stratton enjoys spotting new animals and writing books for children. He lives in Minnesota.

Table of Contents

Many Animals

Many animals have horns.

Animals have horns

on their heads.

Some goats have horns.
Some cows have
horns too.

Some sheep have horns.
Some antelopes have
horns too.

Some lizards have horns.

Some insects do too.

11

Kinds of Horns

Horns can look different.

Some horns are tall, and

some horns are short.

Some horns stand up, and some horns bend down.

Some horns twist up, and some horns curl to the side.

Counting Horns

Some animals have one horn.

Some animals have two horns.

Some rhinos have
one horn.
Some rhinos have
two horns.

Some animals have more
than two horns.
Sheep can have
four horns.

Glossary

antelope

goat

cow

rhino

Index